LEWIS TEWANIMA

LEWIS TEWANIMA
BORN TO RUN

By Sharon K. Solomon
Illustrated by Lisa Fields

PELICAN PUBLISHING COMPANY
Gretna 2014

To Lewis and the eleven other young Hopi men who were taken
from Second Mesa, Arizona in 1906—SS

For my Ino—LF

The word "Pelican" and the depiction of a pelican are
trademarks of Pelican Publishing Company, Inc., and are
registered in the U.S. Patent and Trademark Office.

Library of Congress Cataloging-in-Publication Data

Solomon, Sharon K.
  Lewis Tewanima : born to run / by Sharon K. Solomon ;
illustrated by Lisa Fields.
    pages cm.
  Includes bibliographical references.
  ISBN 978-1-4556-1941-2 (hardcover : alk. paper) — ISBN
978-1-4556-1942-9 (e-book) 1. Tewanima, Lewis 1888-
1969—Juvenile literature. 2. Runners (Sports)—United States—
Biography—Juvenile literature. 3. Olympic athletes—United
States—Biography. 4. Hopi Indians—Biography—Juvenile
literature. I. Fields, Lisa illustrator. II. Title.
  GV1061.15.T49S65 2014
  796.42092—dc23
  [B]
                                      2013036713

Printed in Malaysia
Published by Pelican Publishing Company, Inc.
1000 Burmaster Street, Gretna, Louisiana 70053

Lewis Tewanima loved to run. He ran all the way from his home on Second Mesa to Winslow and back just to watch the trains go by.

That was one hundred twenty miles! Then he climbed the steep stone steps cut into the mesa to reach his village.

Lewis watched the rocks change color as the sun set. His life was in perfect balance.

In his Hopi village of Shungopavi, five hundred feet above the Arizona desert, Lewis had a simple life. He was a farmer, a shepherd, and a member of his mother's antelope clan. Hopi means "peaceful one," and the Hopi people are very peace loving.

Hopis are also very good runners. Lewis had to chase and hunt rabbits, deer, and wild birds. Every day he ran miles from the mesa to his village fields to farm corn, beans, peaches, and squash.

But when Lewis Tewanima was a young man in his twenties, something happened to upset his peaceful, perfect balance. In 1906, the Hopis refused to send their children to government schools.

There was a big fight, and Lewis and eleven other young Hopi men were taken away from their tribe. They were sent to a boarding school in New Mexico to learn American ways. For the first time, Lewis was far away from his beautiful mesa and his family.

Lewis was wearing buckskin clothes and moccasins when he arrived at the school, and he didn't know a word of English. His Hopi clothes were taken away and he had to wear a shirt, trousers, and shoes.

The shoes hurt his feet because he was used to going barefoot or wearing moccasins. His long hair was cut off and he wore it parted in the middle. Lewis and the other Hopis were punished if they spoke Hopi instead of English.

About a year later, in 1907, the twelve young Hopi men were sent to the Carlisle Indian School in Pennsylvania, two thousand miles from their village on Second Mesa. They went from desert to paved streets and sidewalks. At Carlisle, there were young men and women from many Indian tribes.

They all wore uniforms and had to speak English. Here they learned trades like black-smithing, carpentry, or farming and were paid a small amount of money. Lewis studied tailoring. It reminded him of the blankets he wove back home.

Sports were also very important at the Carlisle Indian School. The new coach, Glenn "Pop" Warner, taught football, baseball, basketball, and track. When he met little Lewis Tewanima, who was five foot three inches tall and weighed a little over one hundred pounds, he didn't think Lewis would be good at sports. But Lewis told him, "All Hopis run fast good. Me run fast good." Pop Warner repeated these words to reporters at the time.

So Lewis was given a tracksuit and running shoes. Lewis won many ten- and fifteen- mile races with nearby colleges. Once, he missed the train to a track meet in Harrisburg, so Lewis ran the eighteen miles and then won the race.

Next Lewis won the New Orleans Marathon and the New York Evening Mall Marathon.

When Lewis raced in Madison Square Garden, he was not used to racing on an oval track. He told Coach Warner, "You tell me front man and I'll get him!" Some people called him the fastest man in the world. The newspaper reported, "Little Tewanima Wins Marathon." Then it added that he "demonstrated the superiority of the red man as a foot runner."

There were many fast runners on the Carlisle team. Frank Mt. Pleasant and Lewis sailed to London, England, to compete in the 1908 Olympic Games. Lewis's feet and knees hurt, and he finished the marathon in ninth place. Frank was sixth in the broad jump.

They both did better that summer in Paris, France, where Frank won the broad jump and Lewis came in second in the three-mile race.

When they got home, Lewis and Frank visited President Theodore Roosevelt at his home in New York. The president said that he was "glad to have his country represented by genuine Native Americans." Lewis saw the grandeur of President Roosevelt's home with its fancy furniture and paintings. It was not at all like his clay home on the mesa, which had no electricity or inside toilets. Even so, Lewis missed his beloved mesa.

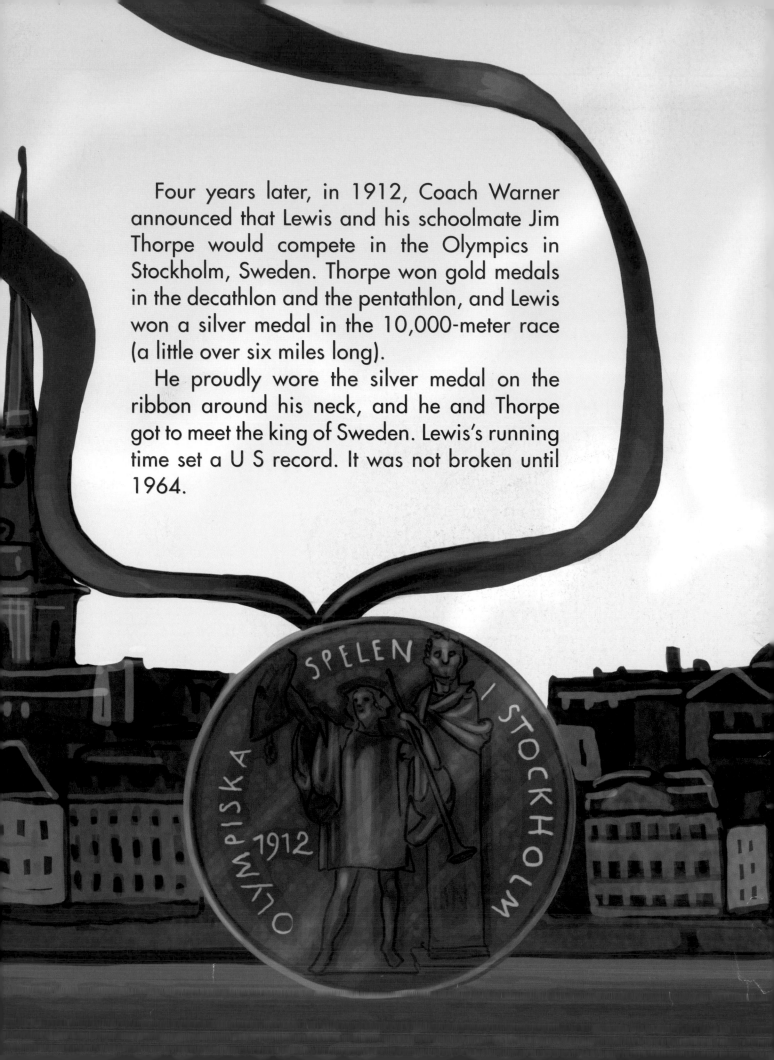

Four years later, in 1912, Coach Warner announced that Lewis and his schoolmate Jim Thorpe would compete in the Olympics in Stockholm, Sweden. Thorpe won gold medals in the decathlon and the pentathlon, and Lewis won a silver medal in the 10,000-meter race (a little over six miles long).

He proudly wore the silver medal on the ribbon around his neck, and he and Thorpe got to meet the king of Sweden. Lewis's running time set a U S record. It was not broken until 1964.

When Lewis and Jim Thorpe got back to the United States, there was a big parade in their honor. They rode with their coach in a horse-drawn carriage through the town of Carlisle, where fifteen thousand people lined the streets. Then, on August 24, one million people came to see them in the New York City victory parade.

Jim Thorpe gave a short speech about his pride in representing the United States. Lewis only said, "Me, too." President William Taft sent a letter of congratulations.

Lewis met a king and a president. He met many famous people and won lots of ribbons and trophies.

But soon after the Olympics, he returned to his village of Shungopavi and lived there for the next fifty-seven years. He went back to his Hopi life on Second Mesa and only left when he was honored.

In 1954, Lewis wore his red headband, purple velvet jacket, white pants, and silver necklace, bracelets, and rings when he flew to New York City to receive the Helms Foundation Award. He was chosen for the All-Time US Olympic Track and Field Team.

In his seventies, Lewis climbed to the top of the Statue of Liberty, looked around New York City, and said, "Not enough land for sheep."

Lewis continued to run even after he returned to Shungopavi. As a Hopi, he believed that he ran not just for himself but for his tribe. That is the Hopi way.

AFTERWORD

Lewis Tewanima died the evening of January 18, 1969. Every Labor Day, his Hopi tribe honors him by holding the Lewis Tewanima Footrace, which begins in his village of Shungopavi. Prizes are given to the fastest runners and money is raised for scholarships for Hopi students.

BIBLIOGRAPHY

Abbey, Edward. *Footrace in the Desert. http://disc.yourwe-bapps.com/discussion.cgi?disc=232051; article=4164.* June 8, 2009.

Banks, Leo. "Lewis Tewanima ran like the wind and is still a hero to young Hopi racers." *Sports Illustrated* online. www.sportsillustrated.cnn.com/vault/article/magazine. MAG1008752/index.htm. September 16, 1996.

Bonvillain, Nancy. *The Hopi Indians of North America.* Philadelphia: Chelsea House, 2005.

Bruchac, Joseph. *Jim Thorpe's Bright Path.* New York: Lee and Low Books, 2004.

Buford, Kate. *Native American Son: The Life and Sporting Legend of Jim Thorpe.* New York: Alfred Knopf, 2010.

Dolan, Edward. *The American Indian Wars.* Brookfield, CT: Millbrook Press, 2003.

Hopi Action News. "Hopi Runner Dies." January 23, 1969.

Hopi Cultural Center, Inc. *A Hopi.* Second Mesa, AZ. 2011.

Hopi Tutuveni (Kykotsmovi, AZ), vol. 18, no. 18. "Lewis Tewanima—Great Hopi Olympic Athlete." August 28, 2008.

Indian Trader (Gallup, NM), vol. 21, no. 1. "Hopi Runner Lewis Tewanima is inducted into Indian Hall of Fame." November 1990.

Indian Trader (Gallup, NM), vol. 27, no. 5. "The Hopi who ran with Jim Thorpe." May 1996.

McDowell, David. "Memories of a Forgotten Hopi Indian." *Hopi Action News.* September 14, 1972.

Murdoch, David. *Eyewitness North American Indian.* New York: DK Publishing, 2005.

New York Times. "Tewanima Defeats Bellars in Match." August 11, 1912.

Oxendine, Joseph B. *American Indian Sports Heritage.* Lincoln: University of Nebraska Press, 1995.

Qua'Toqti (New Oraibi, AZ), vol. 3, no. 6. "Lewis Tewanima Annual Race honors famed Hopi Olympian." 1975: 8-28.

Reavis, Peyton. *Great Little Hopi: Lewis Tewanima.* Tucson: La Prensa Antigua, 1990.

Roosevelt, Theodore. "The Hopi Snake Dance." Chap. 3 in *A Book-Lover's Holidays in the Open,* accessed via www. wordspirituality.org.

LEWIS TEWANIMA TIMELINE

1879	Born in Shungopavi, Second Mesa, Arizona
1906	Hopi uprising Taken to school at Fort Wingate, New Mexico
1907-12	Lives at the Carlisle Indian School, Carlisle, Pennsylvania
1908	Finishes ninth in the marathon at the London, England Olympics
1911	Wins New York Evening Mall Marathon
1912	Wins the Olympic silver medal in the 10,000-meter race Returns to his Hopi village in Arizona and lives as a farmer and shepherd
1918	Carlisle Indian School closes
1920	Wins Mardi Gras race in New Orleans, Louisiana
1954	Chosen for All-Time US Olympic Track and Field Team
1957	Inducted into the Arizona Sports Hall of Fame
1969	Dies on January 18
1972	Inducted into the American Indian Sports Hall of Fame
1974	Annual Lewis Tewanima Memorial Footrace begins